Title of the Book

"Efficient Decision-Making with AI Automation"

By

Ms. Manpreet Kaur

Assistant-Professor

Chandigarh University, Gharuan, Mohali

Preface

- Introduction to the significance of efficient decision-making in various industries.
- Overview of AI automation and its transformative potential.
- Structure of the book and what readers can expect to learn.

Chapter 1: Understanding Decision-Making

- Definition and importance of decision-making in personal and professional contexts.
- Types of decision-making processes: structured vs. unstructured.
- Common challenges faced in decision-making.

Chapter 2: The Fundamentals of Artificial Intelligence

- Overview of AI and its key components: machine learning, natural language processing, etc.
- Types of AI: Narrow AI vs. General AI.
- The role of AI in enhancing decision-making processes.

Chapter 3: The Concept of Automation in Decision-Making

- Definition of automation and its relevance to decision-making.
- Historical context of automation in various industries.
- Benefits of automating decision-making processes.

Chapter 4: AI Techniques for Decision Automation

- Overview of techniques used in AI for decision automation:

- - Rule-based systems
  - Machine learning algorithms
  - Neural networks
  - Bayesian networks
- Case studies illustrate the application of these techniques in real-world scenarios.

Chapter 5: Data-Driven Decision-Making

- Importance of data in AI-driven decision-making.
- Data collection methods and best practices.
- Tools for data analysis and interpretation.

Chapter 6: Challenges and Limitations of AI Automation

- Discussion of common challenges in AI-driven decision-making, including:
  - Data quality and bias
  - Algorithmic transparency
  - Ethical considerations
- Potential solutions to these challenges.

Chapter 7: Implementing AI Automation in Organizations

- Steps for integrating AI automation into existing decision-making processes.
- Best practices for successful implementation.
- Case studies of organizations that have effectively implemented AI automation.

Chapter 8: Future Trends in AI and Decision Automation

- Emerging technologies and their potential impact on decision-making.
- Predictions for the future of AI automation in various sectors.
- The evolving role of human decision-makers in an automated environment.

Conclusion

- Recap of the key concepts discussed throughout the book.
- The importance of embracing AI automation for efficient decision-making.
- Final thoughts on the future of decision-making in the age of AI.

References

- Comprehensive list of academic papers, books, and articles relevant to the topics discussed.

Appendices

- Additional resources for further learning about AI automation and decision-making tools.
- Software and tools for implementing AI-driven decision-making processes.

Preface

In today's fast-paced and data-driven world, the ability to make efficient and informed decisions is critical for success across various industries. From finance and healthcare to manufacturing and retail, organizations are continually faced with complex choices that can significantly impact their operations and outcomes. Efficient decision-making not only enhances productivity but also fosters innovation and competitive advantage.

The advent of artificial intelligence (AI) automation presents a transformative opportunity to optimize decision-making processes. AI technologies have the potential to analyze vast amounts of data, identify patterns, and generate actionable insights far beyond human capabilities. As organizations strive to adapt to rapidly changing environments, embracing AI automation in decision-making becomes essential.

This book aims to provide readers with a thorough understanding of how AI automation can enhance decision-making efficiency. We will explore the foundational concepts of decision-making and AI, delve into various techniques used in automation, and examine the challenges and ethical considerations involved in implementing these technologies.

Structure of the Book:

- Each chapter will build upon the previous one, gradually guiding readers from understanding the basics of decision-making and AI to practical implementation strategies.

- Real-world case studies and best practices will be highlighted to illustrate how organizations successfully integrate AI automation into their decision-making processes.
- We will conclude with future trends and predictions, equipping readers with insights into the evolving landscape of decision-making in the age of AI.

Readers can expect to gain valuable knowledge and practical tools to leverage AI automation in their decision-making processes, ultimately leading to more efficient and informed choices.

Chapter 1: Understanding Decision-Making

Definition and Importance of Decision-Making

Decision-making is the cognitive process of choosing a course of action from among multiple alternatives. This process is fundamental to human functioning and plays a crucial role in both personal and professional contexts. Whether an individual is deciding what to eat for dinner or a company is determining its strategy for the upcoming year, effective decision-making is essential for achieving desired outcomes.

1. **Achieving Goals:** Decision-making enables individuals and organizations to set and achieve objectives. By carefully weighing options, one can align their choices with long-term aspirations.
2. **Solving Problems:** Effective decision-making is vital for identifying and resolving issues. In complex situations, the ability to evaluate different solutions and select the most appropriate one can significantly impact the success of a project or initiative.
3. **Driving Success:** In professional environments, decisions shape business strategies, influence resource allocation, and determine market positioning. Successful decision-making can lead to competitive advantages, increased profitability, and overall organizational effectiveness.

Types of Decision-Making Processes

Decision-making can be categorized into two primary types: structured and unstructured decision-making. Understanding these types is crucial for determining the best approach in different scenarios.

1. **Structured Decision-Making:**
   - **Definition:** Structured decision-making follows a systematic and defined process, often involving quantifiable data and clear criteria for evaluation.
   - **Characteristics:**
     - Uses established methodologies and algorithms.
     - Involves routine or repetitive decisions where past experiences can guide future choices.
     - Examples include financial forecasting, inventory management, and risk assessment.
   - **Advantages:** This approach allows for consistency, repeatability, and efficiency in decision-making, making it easier to analyze outcomes and refine processes over time.

2. **Unstructured Decision-Making:**
   - **Definition:** Unstructured decision-making occurs in ambiguous situations where data may be qualitative rather than quantitative, requiring intuition, creativity, and experience to guide choices.
   - **Characteristics:**
     - Lacks a clear process or defined criteria.
     - Involves complex scenarios that may have far-reaching implications.

- Examples include strategic planning, crisis management, and innovative product development.
    - **Challenges:** Unstructured decision-making can be more subjective, and outcomes may vary based on individual perspectives and biases.

Common Challenges Faced in Decision-Making

Even the most experienced decision-makers encounter challenges that can complicate the decision-making process. Understanding these challenges is critical for developing strategies to mitigate their effects.

1. **Information Overload:**
    - **Description:** In today's data-rich environment, decision-makers often face the challenge of processing vast amounts of information. The abundance of data can make it difficult to identify relevant insights and trends.
    - **Consequences:** Information overload can lead to analysis paralysis, where individuals become overwhelmed by choices and unable to make timely decisions.
2. **Cognitive Biases:**
    - **Description:** Cognitive biases are psychological factors that can distort perception and judgment during the decision-making process. Common biases include confirmation bias (favoring information that confirms pre-existing beliefs)

and anchoring bias (relying too heavily on the first piece of information encountered).
- o **Consequences:** These biases can lead to suboptimal decisions, as individuals may overlook critical data or fail to consider alternative viewpoints.

3. **Time Constraints:**
   - o **Description:** In many situations, decision-makers are under pressure to make quick decisions due to deadlines or changing circumstances. The urgency can inhibit thorough analysis and reflection.
   - o **Consequences:** Rushed decisions can result in errors, missed opportunities, and unfavourable outcomes, particularly in high-stakes environments.

Conclusion of Chapter 1

Understanding the nuances of decision-making is essential for leveraging the power of AI automation effectively. By recognizing the different types of decision-making processes and the common challenges faced, individuals and organizations can better navigate complex choices and prepare for the integration of AI technologies to enhance their decision-making capabilities.

Chapter 2: The Fundamentals of Artificial Intelligence

Overview of AI and Its Key Components

Artificial Intelligence (AI) refers to the simulation of human intelligence in machines that are programmed to think and learn. The primary goal of AI is to enable computers to perform tasks that typically require human intelligence, such as understanding natural language, recognizing patterns, and making decisions. Here are some key components of AI:

1. **Machine Learning (ML):**
   - **Definition:** Machine learning is a subset of AI that involves training algorithms to recognize patterns in data and make predictions or decisions without explicit programming.
   - **Types of Machine Learning:**
     - **Supervised Learning:** Involves training a model on labeled data, allowing it to make predictions based on input-output pairs. Applications include spam detection and image classification.
     - **Unsupervised Learning:** Involves finding patterns or groupings in data without labeled outputs. Applications include customer segmentation and anomaly detection.
     - **Reinforcement Learning:** Involves training an agent to make decisions by rewarding desired outcomes and penalizing undesired ones, commonly used in robotics and gaming.

2. **Natural Language Processing (NLP):**
   - **Definition:** NLP is a branch of AI focused on the interaction between computers and humans through natural language. It enables machines to understand, interpret, and generate human language.
   - **Applications:** NLP powers various applications, including chatbots, sentiment analysis, language translation, and voice recognition systems.

3. **Computer Vision:**
   - **Definition:** Computer vision involves enabling machines to interpret and understand visual information from the world. It encompasses the analysis and processing of images and videos.
   - **Applications:** Common uses include facial recognition, object detection, and autonomous vehicles.

4. **Expert Systems:**
   - **Definition:** Expert systems are AI programs that mimic the decision-making abilities of human experts. They use rule-based logic to solve specific problems within a defined domain.
   - **Applications:** Examples include medical diagnosis systems and troubleshooting guides in technical support.

Types of AI: Narrow AI vs. General AI

Understanding the distinctions between different types of AI is crucial for grasping their capabilities and limitations.

1. **Narrow AI (Weak AI):**
   - **Definition:** Narrow AI refers to AI systems designed to perform specific tasks or solve particular problems. These systems operate within a limited context and lack general cognitive abilities.
   - **Characteristics:**
     - Focused on a single application or a narrow range of tasks.
     - Operates based on pre-defined algorithms and learned patterns from data.
   - **Examples:** Voice assistants (e.g., Siri, Alexa), recommendation systems (e.g., Netflix, Amazon), and fraud detection systems in finance.

2. **General AI (Strong AI):**
   - **Definition:** General AI refers to hypothetical AI systems that possess human-like cognitive abilities and can understand, learn, and apply knowledge across a wide range of tasks.
   - **Characteristics:**
     - Capable of reasoning, problem-solving, and understanding complex concepts.
     - Can transfer knowledge from one domain to another and perform any intellectual task that a human can do.
   - **Current Status:** General AI remains a theoretical concept, and no existing AI systems possess this level of intelligence.

The Role of AI in Enhancing Decision-Making Processes

AI plays a transformative role in enhancing decision-making across various sectors. By automating and augmenting decision processes, AI can lead to improved efficiency, accuracy, and overall outcomes.

1. **Data Analysis and Insights:**
   - AI can process and analyze vast amounts of data quickly, identifying patterns and trends that may be difficult for humans to discern. This capability enables organizations to make informed decisions based on real-time insights.

2. **Predictive Analytics:**
   - AI algorithms can forecast future outcomes based on historical data, allowing decision-makers to anticipate trends and make proactive choices. For instance, businesses can use predictive analytics to optimize inventory levels and minimize stockouts.

3. **Automating Routine Decisions:**
   - By automating routine decision-making processes, AI frees up human resources to focus on more complex and strategic decisions. For example, automated systems can handle customer inquiries or transaction approvals without human intervention.

4. **Enhanced Personalization:**
   - In marketing and customer service, AI-driven systems can analyze customer behavior and preferences, enabling personalized recommendations and targeted campaigns. This level of personalization can significantly improve customer satisfaction and loyalty.

5. **Risk Assessment and Management:**

- AI can help organizations assess risks by analyzing data from various sources, identifying potential threats, and suggesting mitigation strategies. This application is particularly valuable in finance, insurance, and healthcare.

6. **Support for Decision-Makers:**
    - AI tools can serve as decision support systems, providing decision-makers with relevant information, scenarios, and recommendations. By augmenting human judgment, AI can lead to more well-rounded and informed decisions.

Conclusion of Chapter 2

The fundamentals of AI lay the groundwork for understanding how this technology can significantly enhance decision-making processes. By leveraging AI components such as machine learning, natural language processing, and computer vision, organizations can navigate complex choices more efficiently and effectively. As we progress in this book, we will explore how AI automation can be integrated into decision-making to achieve optimal outcomes.

Chapter 3: The Concept of Automation in Decision-Making

Definition of Automation and Its Relevance to Decision-Making

Automation refers to the use of technology to perform tasks with minimal human intervention. It encompasses a wide range of processes, from simple mechanical systems to complex software algorithms that mimic human decision-making. In the context of decision-making, automation can involve the use of AI systems, algorithms, and tools designed to streamline, enhance, or completely replace the human decision-making process.

1. **Relevance to Decision-Making:**
    - **Efficiency:** Automation can significantly reduce the time taken to make decisions by processing data faster than human capabilities.
    - **Consistency:** Automated systems provide a consistent approach to decision-making, reducing variability that may arise from human emotions or biases.
    - **Scalability:** Automated decision-making can handle large volumes of data and transactions, making it feasible for organizations to scale operations without a corresponding increase in human resources.
    - **Focus on Strategic Decisions:** By automating routine decisions, organizations can free up human decision-makers to focus on more complex and strategic issues that require creativity and intuition.

Historical Context of Automation in Various Industries

The concept of automation has evolved significantly over the years, impacting various industries in profound ways.

1. **Early Automation:**
     - The roots of automation can be traced back to the Industrial Revolution in the 18th century, where mechanization began to replace manual labor in manufacturing processes. Simple machines and mechanical devices were created to perform repetitive tasks, improving productivity and efficiency.

2. **Automated Control Systems:**
     - In the mid-20th century, industries began adopting automated control systems for manufacturing processes. Programmable Logic Controllers (PLCs) and early computer systems enabled more sophisticated automation, allowing for real-time monitoring and control of production lines.

3. **Advent of Information Technology:**
     - With the rise of information technology in the 1980s and 1990s, businesses started to automate data processing and administrative tasks. The introduction of enterprise resource planning (ERP) systems allowed organizations to streamline their operations by integrating various functions, including finance, supply chain, and human resources.

4. **AI and Decision Automation:**
     - The past two decades have witnessed significant advancements in AI, leading to the automation of decision-making processes across various sectors. Machine learning algorithms and data analytics tools are now widely used to automate

decisions in areas such as finance (credit scoring), marketing (customer segmentation), and healthcare (diagnostic support).

5. **Emerging Trends:**
    - Currently, industries are embracing emerging technologies such as robotic process automation (RPA), AI-driven decision support systems, and autonomous vehicles. These innovations are transforming the way organizations approach decision-making, leading to increased efficiency and improved outcomes.

Benefits of Automating Decision-Making Processes

The automation of decision-making processes offers a multitude of benefits for organizations, contributing to enhanced performance and competitive advantages.

1. **Increased Efficiency:**
    - Automated systems can process data and make decisions faster than humans, significantly reducing the time required for decision-making. This efficiency is particularly beneficial in high-stakes environments where timely decisions are crucial.

2. **Cost Savings:**
    - By automating routine decisions and processes, organizations can reduce operational costs associated with manual decision-making. Fewer resources are needed to manage these tasks, allowing organizations to allocate their workforce to more strategic activities.

3. **Enhanced Accuracy:**
    - Automated decision-making reduces the likelihood of human errors, such as miscalculations or oversight of critical information. Algorithms can analyze data with precision, leading to more accurate decisions based on factual information.

4. **Improved Data Utilization:**
    - Automation allows organizations to leverage vast amounts of data for decision-making. By integrating data from various sources, automated systems can uncover insights that inform better choices and strategic direction.

5. **Greater Agility:**
    - Automated decision-making enables organizations to respond more quickly to changing market conditions and emerging trends. This agility is crucial in a fast-paced business environment where the ability to pivot and adapt can determine success.

6. **Scalability:**
    - As organizations grow, the volume of decisions required can increase exponentially. Automation allows for the seamless scaling of decision-making processes, enabling organizations to maintain performance levels without a proportional increase in resources.

7. **Enhanced Decision-Making Quality:**
    - By providing decision-makers with data-driven insights and recommendations, automation can improve the overall quality of decisions made. Human decision-makers can leverage these insights to complement their intuition and experience.

Conclusion of Chapter 3

The concept of automation in decision-making is a powerful force that enhances efficiency, accuracy, and strategic focus across various industries. By understanding the historical context and benefits of automated decision-making processes, organizations can better appreciate the transformative potential of AI technologies in driving effective decision-making. As we move forward in this book, we will explore specific AI techniques that facilitate the automation of decision-making and how they can be successfully implemented in organizations.

Chapter 4: AI Techniques for Decision Automation

In this chapter, we explore various AI techniques employed in decision automation. These techniques range from traditional rule-based systems to advanced machine learning algorithms and neural networks. By understanding these methods, organizations can leverage AI to enhance their decision-making processes effectively.

Overview of Techniques Used in AI for Decision Automation

1. **Rule-Based Systems**
   - **Definition:** Rule-based systems use predefined rules to guide decision-making. These rules are typically created by human experts and are based on specific conditions that lead to particular outcomes.
   - **Characteristics:**
     - Simple to implement and understand.
     - Transparent decision-making process.
     - Effective in environments with well-defined rules and low variability.
   - **Applications:** Commonly used in expert systems, such as medical diagnosis tools and troubleshooting guides in customer service. For example, a rule-based system might recommend a specific treatment based on symptoms and patient history.

2. **Machine Learning Algorithms**
   - **Definition:** Machine learning (ML) algorithms enable systems to learn from data and improve their decision-making capabilities over time without explicit programming.
   - **Types of Machine Learning Algorithms:**

- **Supervised Learning:** Models are trained on labeled datasets, allowing them to predict outcomes based on new input data (e.g., regression analysis, decision trees).
- **Unsupervised Learning:** Models identify patterns in unlabeled data (e.g., clustering algorithms like k-means).
- **Reinforcement Learning:** Agents learn through trial and error by receiving rewards or penalties (e.g., Q-learning).
  - **Applications:** ML algorithms are used in fraud detection, recommendation systems, and predictive maintenance. For instance, financial institutions use ML models to detect unusual transaction patterns indicative of fraud.

3. **Neural Networks**
   - **Definition:** Neural networks are a subset of machine learning that mimics the structure and function of the human brain, consisting of interconnected layers of nodes (neurons).
   - **Characteristics:**
     - Capable of processing complex and high-dimensional data.
     - Well-suited for tasks involving image recognition, natural language processing, and speech recognition.
   - **Applications:** Neural networks are widely used in applications such as self-driving cars, image classification, and language translation. For example, convolutional neural networks (CNNs) are employed in facial recognition systems to identify and verify individuals based on their facial features.

4. **Bayesian Networks**

- **Definition:** Bayesian networks are probabilistic graphical models that represent a set of variables and their conditional dependencies using directed acyclic graphs (DAGs).
- **Characteristics:**
  - Useful for modeling uncertainty and incorporating prior knowledge into decision-making.
  - Enable reasoning under uncertainty by updating beliefs based on new evidence (Bayes' theorem).
- **Applications:** Commonly used in medical diagnosis, risk assessment, and decision support systems. For instance, a Bayesian network can help doctors assess the likelihood of a patient having a particular disease based on observed symptoms and prior knowledge about the disease's prevalence.

Case Studies Illustrating the Application of These Techniques in Real-World Scenarios

1. **Case Study: Rule-Based Systems in Medical Diagnosis**
   - **Background:** A leading healthcare provider implemented a rule-based expert system to assist physicians in diagnosing diseases based on patient symptoms and medical history.
   - **Outcome:** The system improved diagnostic accuracy by providing recommendations based on a comprehensive set of rules derived from clinical guidelines. Physicians reported increased confidence in their diagnoses, leading to better patient outcomes.

2. **Case Study: Machine Learning in Fraud Detection**
    - **Background:** A large financial institution deployed machine learning algorithms to monitor transaction patterns and detect potential fraud.
    - **Outcome:** By analyzing historical transaction data, the ML models identified suspicious activities with high accuracy. The implementation of these algorithms reduced fraudulent transactions by over 30% and minimized losses for the organization.

3. **Case Study: Neural Networks for Image Recognition**
    - **Background:** An e-commerce company used convolutional neural networks (CNNs) to automate the process of product categorization based on images uploaded by users.
    - **Outcome:** The neural network model achieved high accuracy in classifying products, significantly reducing the manual effort required for categorization. This automation improved user experience by providing faster search results and relevant recommendations.

4. **Case Study: Bayesian Networks in Risk Assessment**
    - **Background:** An insurance company utilized Bayesian networks to evaluate risks associated with policyholders and determine appropriate premium rates.
    - **Outcome:** By incorporating prior knowledge about risk factors and continuously updating probabilities with new data, the Bayesian network provided more accurate risk assessments. This approach led to optimized pricing strategies and improved profitability for the insurer.

Conclusion of Chapter 4

The various AI techniques outlined in this chapter play a crucial role in automating decision-making processes across different industries. By understanding and leveraging these methods, organizations can enhance their decision-making capabilities, improve efficiency, and achieve better outcomes. As we continue in this book, we will explore the importance of data-driven decision-making and the role of data analysis in successful AI implementation.

Chapter 5: Data-Driven Decision-Making

In today's digital age, data has become a critical asset for organizations striving to make informed decisions. This chapter delves into the importance of data in AI-driven decision-making, explores effective data collection methods and best practices, and highlights tools for data analysis and interpretation.

Importance of Data in AI-Driven Decision-Making

1. **Foundation for Insights:**
   - Data serves as the backbone of AI-driven decision-making. Accurate and relevant data provides the basis for generating insights, identifying patterns, and making predictions that inform strategic choices.

2. **Enhanced Accuracy:**
   - Decisions based on data are typically more accurate and reliable than those based solely on intuition or anecdotal evidence. By leveraging data analytics, organizations can minimize biases and errors in their decision-making processes.

3. **Real-Time Decision-Making:**
   - With the ability to collect and analyze data in real time, organizations can respond quickly to emerging trends and changes in the market. This agility is crucial for maintaining a competitive edge.

4. **Predictive Capabilities:**
   - Data-driven approaches enable organizations to use historical data to forecast future outcomes. This predictive capability allows businesses to anticipate challenges and seize opportunities proactively.

5. **Continuous Improvement:**
    - Data allows organizations to evaluate the effectiveness of their decisions over time. By analyzing the outcomes of past decisions, businesses can refine their strategies and improve their decision-making frameworks.

Data Collection Methods and Best Practices

1. **Data Collection Methods:**
    - **Surveys and Questionnaires:** Gathering information directly from customers or stakeholders can provide valuable insights into preferences, behaviors, and satisfaction levels.
    - **Interviews and Focus Groups:** Conducting one-on-one interviews or group discussions can yield qualitative data that deepens understanding of user needs and motivations.
    - **Web Analytics:** Tools like Google Analytics allow organizations to track user interactions on websites, providing insights into customer behavior and preferences.
    - **Social Media Monitoring:** Analyzing social media platforms can reveal public sentiment and trends related to products, services, or brands.
    - **Transactional Data:** Collecting data from sales transactions, customer interactions, and other business processes provides quantitative insights for decision-making.

- **IoT Devices:** Internet of Things (IoT) devices can collect real-time data from various sources, such as sensors in manufacturing or smart home devices.

2. **Best Practices for Data Collection:**
    - **Define Clear Objectives:** Before collecting data, organizations should establish clear goals to guide the data collection process and ensure relevance.
    - **Ensure Data Quality:** Prioritize accuracy, completeness, and consistency in data collection. Implement validation techniques to minimize errors.
    - **Consider Privacy and Ethics:** Ensure compliance with data protection regulations and ethical standards when collecting and handling data, particularly personal information.
    - **Utilize Diverse Sources:** Employ a combination of qualitative and quantitative data sources to gain a comprehensive understanding of the decision-making context.
    - **Regularly Review and Update Data:** Data should be regularly reviewed and updated to ensure it remains relevant and accurate, reflecting current trends and conditions.

Tools for Data Analysis and Interpretation

1. **Data Analysis Tools:**
    - **Spreadsheet Software (e.g., Microsoft Excel, Google Sheets):** Widely used for basic data analysis, including statistical functions, data visualization, and pivot tables.

- **Statistical Software (e.g., R, SAS, SPSS):** These tools offer advanced statistical analysis capabilities, enabling organizations to perform complex data modeling and hypothesis testing.
- **Business Intelligence (BI) Tools (e.g., Tableau, Power BI):** BI tools facilitate data visualization and dashboard creation, allowing users to analyze data and identify trends easily.
- **Machine Learning Frameworks (e.g., TensorFlow, Scikit-learn):** These frameworks provide tools for building, training, and deploying machine learning models, enabling predictive analytics and automated decision-making.
- **Database Management Systems (e.g., SQL, NoSQL databases):** These systems allow for efficient data storage, retrieval, and manipulation, ensuring organizations can access and analyze large datasets.

2. **Interpretation Tools:**
   - **Data Visualization Software:** Tools such as Tableau or Google Data Studio help create visual representations of data, making complex information more accessible and understandable.
   - **Natural Language Processing (NLP) Tools:** NLP techniques can analyze text data from sources like customer feedback, social media, and surveys, providing insights into customer sentiments and opinions.
   - **AI-Powered Analytics Platforms:** Solutions like IBM Watson Analytics or Google AI provide advanced capabilities for analyzing data and generating insights through natural language queries and automated analysis.

Conclusion of Chapter 5

Data-driven decision-making is essential for organizations aiming to thrive in a competitive landscape. By understanding the importance of data, employing effective collection methods, and utilizing the right analysis tools, organizations can enhance their decision-making processes. The subsequent chapters will explore the challenges and limitations of AI automation, along with best practices for implementing AI-driven solutions in organizations.

Chapter 6: Challenges and Limitations of AI Automation

As organizations increasingly turn to AI for automating decision-making processes, they encounter various challenges and limitations. Understanding these issues is essential for ensuring the effective and responsible implementation of AI technologies. This chapter discusses some common challenges in AI-driven decision-making and explores potential solutions.

Common Challenges in AI-Driven Decision-Making

1. **Data Quality and Bias**
   - **Data Quality:**
     - The effectiveness of AI algorithms heavily relies on the quality of data used for training. Poor-quality data—characterized by inaccuracies, inconsistencies, and incompleteness—can lead to flawed decision-making.
     - For instance, if the data used to train a model is outdated or lacks diversity, the model may produce irrelevant or incorrect results.
   - **Bias in Data:**
     - Data bias occurs when the training data reflects societal prejudices or stereotypes, resulting in algorithms that reinforce these biases in their decision-making.
     - For example, an AI recruitment tool trained on historical hiring data might inadvertently favor candidates from specific demographics, perpetuating inequality.
2. **Algorithmic Transparency**
   - **Lack of Interpretability:**

- Many advanced AI models, particularly deep learning algorithms, operate as "black boxes," making it difficult for users to understand how decisions are made.
- This lack of transparency raises concerns about accountability and trust, as stakeholders may be hesitant to rely on systems whose decision-making processes are not easily interpretable.

- **Regulatory Compliance:**
  - As regulations around AI and data usage tighten, organizations face pressure to provide transparency in their algorithms. Meeting these requirements can be challenging when models are complex and hard to explain.

3. **Ethical Considerations**

   - **Ethical Dilemmas:**
     - The use of AI in decision-making can lead to ethical dilemmas, particularly in sensitive areas such as healthcare, criminal justice, and hiring practices. Decisions made by AI systems can have profound impacts on individuals' lives, raising questions about fairness and justice.

   - **Job Displacement:**
     - As AI automates more decision-making processes, there are concerns about job displacement for human workers. The transition to AI-driven systems may result in significant workforce changes, requiring retraining and upskilling efforts.

Potential Solutions to These Challenges

1. **Enhancing Data Quality and Addressing Bias**
   - **Data Validation and Cleaning:**
     - Implement data validation processes to ensure the accuracy and completeness of the datasets used for training AI models. Regularly cleaning and updating data can mitigate issues related to data quality.
   - **Diverse Data Sources:**
     - Utilize diverse data sources to train models, ensuring that the training data represents a broad range of perspectives and demographics. This approach can help reduce bias and improve the fairness of AI systems.
   - **Bias Detection Tools:**
     - Employ tools and techniques for detecting and mitigating bias in AI models. For instance, organizations can conduct audits to identify biases and use fairness-enhancing interventions during the model training phase.

2. **Promoting Algorithmic Transparency**
   - **Explainable AI (XAI):**
     - Invest in research and development of explainable AI techniques that improve the interpretability of AI models. Techniques such as LIME (Local Interpretable Model-agnostic Explanations) and SHAP (SHapley Additive exPlanations) can help provide insights into how models make decisions.
   - **Documentation and Reporting:**

- Maintain comprehensive documentation of AI models, including their design, training data, and decision-making processes. This documentation can facilitate regulatory compliance and enhance stakeholder trust.
    - **User Training:**
        - Provide training for users and stakeholders on how AI systems work and their limitations. Educating users about AI can help build trust and understanding of the technology.

3. **Addressing Ethical Considerations**
    - **Ethical Guidelines and Frameworks:**
        - Develop and adopt ethical guidelines for the use of AI in decision-making. These guidelines should prioritize fairness, accountability, and transparency, ensuring that AI systems operate within ethical boundaries.
    - **Stakeholder Engagement:**
        - Involve diverse stakeholders in the design and implementation of AI systems, including representatives from affected communities. Engaging stakeholders can help identify ethical concerns and ensure that AI technologies serve the public good.
    - **Reskilling and Workforce Transition:**
        - Invest in reskilling and training programs for employees affected by automation. Preparing the workforce for the changing landscape can mitigate job displacement and ensure that human workers remain integral to decision-making processes.

Conclusion of Chapter 6

While AI automation holds immense potential for enhancing decision-making processes, it is not without challenges and limitations. By recognizing issues related to data quality, algorithmic transparency, and ethical considerations, organizations can proactively address these challenges and leverage AI responsibly. The subsequent chapters will explore practical strategies for implementing AI automation in organizations and the future trends shaping the landscape of decision-making.

Chapter 7: Implementing AI Automation in Organizations

The successful integration of AI automation into decision-making processes can transform an organization's operational efficiency and strategic capabilities. This chapter outlines the essential steps for integrating AI automation, shares best practices for implementation, and presents case studies of organizations that have effectively leveraged AI technologies.

Steps for Integrating AI Automation into Existing Decision-Making Processes

1. **Identify Business Objectives:**
    - Clearly define the specific goals and objectives that AI automation aims to achieve. This could include enhancing decision accuracy, improving operational efficiency, or reducing costs.
    - Align AI initiatives with the organization's overall strategy to ensure that automation contributes to broader business objectives.

2. **Assess Current Processes:**
    - Conduct a thorough analysis of existing decision-making processes to identify inefficiencies, bottlenecks, and areas where automation could provide value.
    - Evaluate the types of decisions made, the data sources used, and the stakeholders involved in these processes.

3. **Select Appropriate AI Technologies:**
    - Based on the identified objectives and current processes, choose the appropriate AI technologies and tools that best fit the organization's needs.

- Consider factors such as data availability, technical feasibility, and organizational readiness when selecting technologies (e.g., machine learning algorithms, natural language processing, etc.).

4. **Develop a Pilot Project:**
   - Start with a pilot project to test the integration of AI automation on a smaller scale. This allows organizations to evaluate the effectiveness of the technology in a controlled environment.
   - Set clear success metrics for the pilot project to measure its impact and identify any necessary adjustments.

5. **Gather and Prepare Data:**
   - Ensure that high-quality, relevant data is available for training AI models. This may involve cleaning, validating, and integrating data from various sources.
   - Collaborate with data experts to establish data governance practices that ensure data integrity and compliance.

6. **Build and Train AI Models:**
   - Develop and train AI models using the prepared data. This may involve selecting algorithms, tuning parameters, and conducting validation tests to ensure accuracy.
   - Collaborate with data scientists and AI experts to optimize the models for specific decision-making scenarios.

7. **Implement and Monitor:**
   - Deploy the AI models into the existing decision-making processes, ensuring seamless integration with current workflows.

- Continuously monitor the performance of the AI systems and gather feedback from users to identify areas for improvement.

8. **Scale and Optimize:**
    - Once the pilot project demonstrates success, scale the implementation to other areas of the organization.
    - Continuously optimize AI models and decision-making processes based on performance data and user feedback.

Best Practices for Successful Implementation

1. **Foster a Culture of Innovation:**
    - Encourage a culture that embraces innovation and experimentation within the organization. This mindset helps alleviate resistance to change and promotes the acceptance of AI technologies.

2. **Engage Stakeholders Early:**
    - Involve key stakeholders, including employees and management, early in the implementation process to ensure buy-in and support.
    - Solicit their input and feedback throughout the project to foster a sense of ownership and collaboration.

3. **Provide Training and Support:**
    - Offer training programs to equip employees with the skills needed to work alongside AI technologies effectively. This includes technical training as well as education on how to interpret AI-generated insights.

- Provide ongoing support to address any concerns or challenges that arise during the integration process.

4. **Prioritize Ethical Considerations:**
    - Ensure that ethical considerations are integrated into the AI implementation process. This includes establishing guidelines for fairness, transparency, and accountability in AI decision-making.
    - Regularly review and assess the ethical implications of AI technologies in practice.

5. **Establish Robust Governance:**
    - Develop a governance framework that outlines roles, responsibilities, and processes for managing AI systems within the organization.
    - This framework should include data governance, risk management, and compliance with regulatory requirements.

Case Studies of Organizations that Have Effectively Implemented AI Automation

1. **Case Study: Google – AI-Driven Decision-Making in Advertising**
    - **Background:** Google has integrated AI technologies into its advertising platform, utilizing machine learning algorithms to optimize ad placements and targeting.
    - **Outcome:** By automating ad bidding and targeting decisions, Google has increased the effectiveness of its advertising campaigns, resulting in improved customer engagement and higher revenue for advertisers.

2. **Case Study: Siemens – Predictive Maintenance in Manufacturing**

- **Background:** Siemens implemented AI automation for predictive maintenance in its manufacturing plants, using data from sensors to predict equipment failures.
- **Outcome:** This approach has significantly reduced downtime and maintenance costs while increasing operational efficiency, allowing Siemens to improve production schedules and overall performance.

3. **Case Study: Netflix – Content Recommendation System**
   - **Background:** Netflix employs AI algorithms to analyze user viewing habits and preferences to recommend personalized content.
   - **Outcome:** This AI-driven recommendation system has enhanced user engagement and satisfaction, contributing to Netflix's growth in subscriber numbers and retention rates.

4. **Case Study: Zocdoc – Streamlining Patient Booking**
   - **Background:** Zocdoc utilized AI automation to streamline its patient booking process, allowing users to find and book medical appointments based on their preferences and availability.
   - **Outcome:** The implementation of AI has simplified the user experience, leading to increased appointment bookings and higher patient satisfaction rates.

Conclusion of Chapter 7

Integrating AI automation into decision-making processes offers organizations the opportunity to enhance efficiency and improve outcomes. By following the outlined steps, adhering to best practices, and learning from successful case studies, organizations can effectively navigate the complexities of AI implementation. In the next chapter, we will explore future trends in AI and decision automation, highlighting emerging technologies and their potential impact on the decision-making landscape.

Chapter 8: Future Trends in AI and Decision Automation

As artificial intelligence (AI) continues to evolve, its integration into decision-making processes is expected to transform various sectors significantly. This chapter explores emerging technologies, predictions for the future of AI automation across industries, and the evolving role of human decision-makers in an increasingly automated environment.

Emerging Technologies and Their Potential Impact on Decision-Making

1. **Explainable AI (XAI):**
    - **Definition:** Explainable AI aims to make AI decision-making processes transparent and understandable to users.
    - **Impact:** As organizations adopt XAI, decision-makers will gain insights into how AI arrives at its conclusions, fostering trust and enabling better collaboration between humans and machines.
2. **Edge Computing:**
    - **Definition:** Edge computing involves processing data closer to its source rather than relying on centralized cloud servers.
    - **Impact:** By reducing latency, edge computing allows for real-time data analysis and faster decision-making, particularly in sectors like manufacturing, healthcare, and autonomous vehicles.
3. **Natural Language Processing (NLP) Advancements:**

- **Definition:** NLP focuses on the interaction between computers and human language, enabling machines to understand, interpret, and generate human language.
- **Impact:** Improved NLP capabilities will enhance decision-making by facilitating better communication and collaboration between AI systems and human users, particularly in customer service and content generation.

4. **Quantum Computing:**
   - **Definition:** Quantum computing leverages the principles of quantum mechanics to perform calculations at unprecedented speeds.
   - **Impact:** Quantum computing has the potential to revolutionize decision-making in fields such as finance and logistics, allowing for the analysis of vast datasets and complex models that were previously impractical.

5. **Autonomous Systems:**
   - **Definition:** Autonomous systems are capable of making decisions without human intervention, using AI algorithms to navigate and respond to their environments.
   - **Impact:** Industries such as transportation, agriculture, and healthcare are likely to see increased efficiency and reduced human error through the implementation of autonomous systems.

Predictions for the Future of AI Automation in Various Sectors

1. **Healthcare:**

- **Prediction:** AI will enable more personalized medicine, utilizing patient data to recommend tailored treatment plans and improve diagnostic accuracy.
- **Impact:** Decision-making in healthcare will become more data-driven, leading to better patient outcomes and more efficient resource allocation.

2. **Finance:**
    - **Prediction:** AI automation will enhance fraud detection, risk assessment, and algorithmic trading, resulting in faster and more accurate financial decision-making.
    - **Impact:** Financial institutions will rely heavily on AI-driven insights to make informed investment decisions and manage risks effectively.

3. **Manufacturing:**
    - **Prediction:** The adoption of AI and automation will lead to the rise of smart factories, where machines make real-time decisions based on data from production lines.
    - **Impact:** This shift will optimize production processes, reduce waste, and enhance supply chain management.

4. **Retail:**
    - **Prediction:** AI will increasingly personalize customer experiences through predictive analytics and targeted marketing, influencing purchasing decisions.
    - **Impact:** Retailers will harness AI to streamline inventory management, enhance customer engagement, and optimize pricing strategies.

5. **Transportation:**

- **Prediction:** AI will facilitate the growth of autonomous vehicles, reshaping urban mobility and logistics.
- **Impact:** Decision-making in transportation will increasingly rely on AI algorithms to optimize routes, improve safety, and enhance overall efficiency.

The Evolving Role of Human Decision-Makers in an Automated Environment

1. **Collaborative Decision-Making:**
   - As AI systems become more integrated into decision-making processes, the role of human decision-makers will shift towards collaboration with AI. Humans will need to interpret AI-generated insights, assess their relevance, and make informed choices based on a combination of human intuition and machine intelligence.

2. **Focus on Complex Problem-Solving:**
   - Human decision-makers will be tasked with addressing more complex, unstructured problems that require emotional intelligence, creativity, and ethical considerations—areas where AI currently falls short. This evolution will emphasize the need for humans to engage in strategic thinking and innovative problem-solving.

3. **Ethical Oversight:**
   - With the increased reliance on AI, human decision-makers will play a crucial role in ensuring ethical practices in AI implementation. This includes evaluating AI decisions for fairness, accountability, and transparency, and making adjustments as necessary to uphold organizational values.

4. **Continuous Learning and Adaptation:**
    - As AI technologies advance, human decision-makers will need to embrace continuous learning and adaptability to remain effective in their roles. This may involve acquiring new skills related to data analysis, AI interpretation, and the ethical implications of automated decision-making.
5. **Interdisciplinary Collaboration:**
    - The future will demand greater collaboration among various disciplines, including data science, ethics, and domain-specific expertise. Human decision-makers will be essential in bridging these areas to ensure that AI solutions are well-informed, contextually relevant, and aligned with organizational goals.

Conclusion of Chapter 8

The future of AI and decision automation holds tremendous promise, with emerging technologies poised to revolutionize how organizations make decisions. As sectors adapt to these changes, the role of human decision-makers will evolve, requiring a focus on collaboration, ethical oversight, and continuous learning. Embracing these trends will empower organizations to leverage AI effectively and enhance decision-making processes for improved outcomes.

Conclusion

In this book, we have explored the transformative power of AI automation in decision-making across various industries. Here's a recap of the key concepts discussed throughout the chapters:

1. **Understanding Decision-Making:**
    - We defined decision-making and its importance in both personal and professional contexts, distinguishing between structured and unstructured decision-making processes. The challenges of information overload, cognitive biases, and time constraints were also addressed.

2. **The Fundamentals of Artificial Intelligence:**
    - An overview of AI was provided, highlighting key components such as machine learning and natural language processing. We differentiated between Narrow AI and General AI, emphasizing the role of AI in enhancing decision-making.

3. **The Concept of Automation in Decision-Making:**
    - The definition of automation and its relevance was discussed, along with the historical context of automation across industries and the benefits of automating decision-making processes.

4. **AI Techniques for Decision Automation:**
    - Various techniques for decision automation, including rule-based systems, machine learning algorithms, neural networks, and Bayesian networks, were explored, supported by real-world case studies demonstrating their application.

5. **Data-Driven Decision-Making:**

- o   We emphasized the importance of data in AI-driven decision-making, discussing best practices for data collection and tools for data analysis and interpretation.

6. **Challenges and Limitations of AI Automation:**
    - o   Common challenges such as data quality, algorithmic transparency, and ethical considerations were examined, along with potential solutions to these challenges.

7. **Implementing AI Automation in Organizations:**
    - o   We outlined steps for integrating AI automation into existing decision-making processes, best practices for successful implementation, and case studies of organizations that have effectively leveraged AI technologies.

8. **Future Trends in AI and Decision Automation:**
    - o   Emerging technologies and their impact on decision-making were discussed, alongside predictions for AI automation in various sectors and the evolving role of human decision-makers in an automated environment.

The Importance of Embracing AI Automation for Efficient Decision-Making

The integration of AI automation into decision-making processes is not merely a trend; it represents a fundamental shift in how organizations operate. By embracing AI, organizations can streamline their processes, enhance accuracy, and make informed decisions that drive success. The synergy between human insight and AI capabilities will be pivotal in navigating complex challenges and unlocking new opportunities.

Final Thoughts on the Future of Decision-Making in the Age of AI

As we move further into the age of AI, the landscape of decision-making will continue to evolve. Organizations that prioritize adaptability, ethical considerations, and continuous learning will be better positioned to harness the potential of AI automation. The future of decision-making will likely be characterized by a collaborative approach, where human intuition complements AI-driven insights, leading to more informed, effective, and ethical decisions.

References

- **Russell, S., & Norvig, P.** (2020). *Artificial Intelligence: A Modern Approach* (4th ed.). Pearson Education.

  - A foundational text on AI that covers both theoretical concepts and practical applications in AI, decision-making, and automation.

- **Goodfellow, I., Bengio, Y., & Courville, A.** (2016). *Deep Learning*. MIT Press.

  - A detailed exploration of deep learning, which plays a critical role in AI decision-making systems.

- **Silver, D., Huang, A., Maddison, C. J., et al.** (2016). "Mastering the Game of Go with Deep Neural Networks and Tree Search." *Nature*, 529(7587), 484-489. doi:10.1038/nature16961

  - This paper demonstrates how AI systems like AlphaGo use deep learning and search algorithms to make complex decisions in real time.

- **Kahneman, D.** (2011). *Thinking, Fast and Slow*. Farrar, Straus and Giroux.

- Although not specifically about AI, this book delves into human decision-making processes, offering valuable insight into how AI models can mimic or enhance human cognitive processes.

- **Bostrom, N.** (2014). *Superintelligence: Paths, Dangers, Strategies*. Oxford University Press.

  - A comprehensive examination of the implications of advanced AI on decision-making, ethics, and future technological developments.

- **Sutton, R. S., & Barto, A. G.** (2018). *Reinforcement Learning: An Introduction* (2nd ed.). MIT Press.

  - A deep dive into reinforcement learning, a method through which AI systems learn to make optimal decisions in dynamic environments.

- **Gerd Gigerenzer** (2007). *Gut Feelings: The Intelligence of the Unconscious*. Penguin Books.

  - A study on decision-making based on heuristics, offering a contrasting view of AI's data-driven approaches versus intuitive human decisions.

- **Mitchell, T. M.** (1997). *Machine Learning*. McGraw Hill.

  - A classic textbook that outlines the principles of machine learning, which are essential for developing AI systems that can automate decision-making.

- **Tversky, A., & Kahneman, D.** (1974). "Judgment under Uncertainty: Heuristics and Biases." *Science*, 185(4157), 1124-1131. doi:10.1126/science.185.4157.1124

- This influential paper discusses human cognitive biases and heuristics, providing insight into how AI systems can counter or replicate these biases.

- **Simon, H. A.** (1972). "Theories of Bounded Rationality." In *Decision and Organization*, 161-176. North-Holland.

  - A classic work on decision-making, which highlights the limitations of human rationality and how AI can enhance decision-making processes by expanding cognitive capabilities.

- **Brynjolfsson, E., & McAfee, A.** (2014). *The Second Machine Age: Work, Progress, and Prosperity in a Time of Brilliant Technologies.* W.W. Norton & Company.

  - A broader look at AI and automation's impact on society, with a focus on how these technologies influence decision-making in economic and organizational contexts.

- **Shrestha, Y. R., & Yang, Y.** (2019). "Fairness in Algorithmic Decision-Making: An Interdisciplinary Review." *Journal of Information Technology*, 34(3), 1-24.

  - A contemporary review of fairness and ethical concerns in AI decision-making systems.

- **Rao, A. S., & Georgeff, M. P.** (1995). "BDI Agents: From Theory to Practice." *Proceedings of the First International Conference on Multi-Agent Systems (ICMAS-95)*, 312-319.

  - A key paper discussing the Belief-Desire-Intention (BDI) model, relevant to AI agents used in autonomous decision-making.

- **Bourgine, P., & Lespérance, Y.** (Eds.). (2004). *Autonomous Agents and Multi-Agent Systems*. Springer.

- A collection of research papers focused on how autonomous agents work together to make decisions in complex, multi-agent environments.

- **Müller, V. C.** (Ed.). (2016). *Risks of Artificial Intelligence*. CRC Press.

  - A critical examination of the risks associated with AI-driven decision-making, including ethical, legal, and safety considerations.

- **Floridi, L., & Cowls, J.** (2019). "A Unified Framework of Five Principles for AI in Society." *Harvard Data Science Review*, 1(1). doi:10.1162/99608f92.8cd550d1

  - This paper outlines a comprehensive framework for guiding the ethical use of AI in decision-making contexts.

- **Agrawal, A., Gans, J., & Goldfarb, A.** (2018). *Prediction Machines: The Simple Economics of Artificial Intelligence*. Harvard Business Review Press.

  - A practical guide to understanding how AI, particularly predictive algorithms, is transforming decision-making in business and economics.

- **Russell, S.** (2019). *Human Compatible: Artificial Intelligence and the Problem of Control*. Viking.

  - A discussion on ensuring AI systems remain aligned with human values, especially in automated decision-making scenarios.

Academic Papers

1. **Russell, S., & Norvig, P.** (2021). *Artificial Intelligence: A Modern Approach* (4th ed.). Prentice Hall.
   - A fundamental text on AI, covering a broad range of topics including AI decision-making systems.
2. **Kahneman, D., & Tversky, A.** (1979). Prospect theory: An analysis of decision under risk. *Econometrica*, 47(2), 263–291.
   - Seminal work on decision theory, valuable for understanding human decision-making biases, relevant when comparing with AI systems.
3. **Sutton, R. S., & Barto, A. G.** (2018). *Reinforcement Learning: An Introduction* (2nd ed.). MIT Press.
   - Detailed exploration of reinforcement learning, a key area of AI impacting autonomous decision-making.
4. **Silver, D., et al.** (2016). Mastering the game of Go with deep neural networks and tree search. *Nature*, 529(7587), 484-489.
   - A landmark paper in AI, illustrating how deep learning models make complex decisions.

Books

1. **Shapiro, C., & Varian, H. R.** (1998). *Information Rules: A Strategic Guide to the Network Economy*. Harvard Business Review Press.
   - Offers insight into how decision-making and strategy are affected by the digital economy, relevant to AI applications.

2. **Brynjolfsson, E., & McAfee, A.** (2014). *The Second Machine Age: Work, Progress, and Prosperity in a Time of Brilliant Technologies.* W. W. Norton & Company.
    - Discusses how AI and automation impact the economy and decision-making in industries.
3. **Tetlock, P. E., & Gardner, D.** (2015). *Superforecasting: The Art and Science of Prediction.* Crown Publishing Group.
    - Focuses on decision-making and predictive analytics, linking human forecasting and AI decision systems.

Articles

1. **Bostrom, N.** (2014). Ethical issues in advanced AI. *Philosophy Now*, 53(1), 46-51.
    - Explores ethical challenges associated with AI making critical decisions autonomously.
2. **Mittelstadt, B. D., Allo, P., Taddeo, M., Wachter, S., & Floridi, L.** (2016). The ethics of algorithms: Mapping the debate. *Big Data & Society*, 3(2), 2053951716679679.
    - Discusses the ethical dimensions of AI-driven decision-making processes.
3. **Amodei, D., et al.** (2016). Concrete problems in AI safety. *arXiv preprint arXiv:1606.06565.*
    - Investigates safety challenges in the development of autonomous systems.

Reports

1. **McKinsey & Company** (2018). *AI, automation, and the future of work.*
    - Highlights how automation influences decision-making in various industries.

2. **World Economic Forum** (2020). *Artificial Intelligence in Finance.*
   - Analyzes the role of AI in financial decision-making and its transformative impact on the sector.

Appendices

Appendix A: Software and Tools for AI-Driven Decision-Making

1. Data Analysis and Visualization Tools

- **Tableau**
  - **Description:** A leading data visualization tool that allows users to create interactive and shareable dashboards. It integrates with various data sources and uses AI to enhance analytics.
  - **Applications:** Business intelligence, performance metrics tracking, data storytelling.
- **Power BI**
  - **Description:** Microsoft's analytics service that provides interactive visualizations and business intelligence capabilities. It features AI-driven insights to aid decision-making.
  - **Applications:** Reporting, dashboard creation, and real-time data analysis.

2. Machine Learning Platforms

- **Google Cloud AI Platform**
  - **Description:** A comprehensive suite of tools for building, deploying, and managing machine learning models. It includes tools for data preparation, model training, and evaluation.
  - **Applications:** Predictive analytics, natural language processing, image analysis.
- **Amazon SageMaker**
  - **Description:** A fully managed service that provides every developer and data scientist with the ability to build, train, and deploy machine learning models quickly.
  - **Applications:** Automated model tuning, deployment, and monitoring.

3. Decision Support Systems

- **IBM Watson Studio**
  - **Description:** A collaborative environment for data scientists, application developers, and subject matter experts to work with data. It includes tools for building AI models and applications.
  - **Applications:** Data analysis, model building, and decision-making support.
- **Microsoft Azure Machine Learning**
  - **Description:** A cloud-based environment for developing and deploying machine learning models. It offers automated machine learning and pre-built algorithms.
  - **Applications:** Workflow automation, model management, and operationalization of ML solutions.

4. Business Process Automation Tools

- **UiPath**
  - **Description:** A leading robotic process automation (RPA) platform that allows businesses to automate repetitive tasks. It integrates AI capabilities for enhanced decision-making.
  - **Applications:** Workflow automation, data extraction, and reporting.
- **Zapier**
  - **Description:** A tool that automates tasks between web apps. It allows users to connect different applications and automate workflows with minimal coding.
  - **Applications:** Task automation, integration of applications, and workflow optimization.

5. Natural Language Processing Tools

- **OpenAI GPT-3**
  - **Description:** An advanced language model that can generate human-like text, which can be used for content creation, chatbots, and data analysis.
  - **Applications:** Automated reporting, customer service automation, and content generation.
- **Microsoft Azure Text Analytics**
  - **Description:** A cloud service that provides advanced natural language processing over raw text, including sentiment analysis, key phrase extraction, and language detection.
  - **Applications:** Customer feedback analysis, social media monitoring, and content optimization.

Conclusion

This appendix provides a comprehensive list of software solutions and tools that organizations can leverage to integrate AI automation into their decision-making workflows. By utilizing these tools, businesses can enhance their analytical capabilities, streamline operations, and improve decision quality.

This book aims to equip readers with the knowledge and insights needed to navigate the complexities of decision-making in the age of AI. Embracing these advancements will be essential for individuals and organizations seeking to thrive in an increasingly automated world.